Strength of Wild Horses

Exclusive Kickstarter Bookplate

The Strength of Wild Horses

Written by

Sandra Tayler

Illustrated by

Angela Call

For information contact:
The Tayler Corporation
PO Box 385
Orem UT 84057

Additional information available at holdontoyourhorses.com

ISBN 978-0-9835746-6-8
First printing April 2014
Printed in China

Amy was a girl
with ideas like wild horses.

Amy tried to control her ideas
and steer them in good directions.

But they ran fast
and going fast was fun.

When the run was over,
there was Amy,
and the mess.

People got mad
at her a lot,

especially her sister, Kari.

One morning an idea horse woke Amy early to write better words for all the songs she knew.

Amy sang as quietly as she could.
She even wore headphones.

Kari got mad anyway.

Later that morning a tiny horse led Amy on a **giant** adventure using all the stuffed animals in the house.

She tried to include Evan,

but he just cried because she had
his **favorite bear.**

Kari scowled,
and took back all her stuffed animals.

In the afternoon another horse prompted Amy to make a **safari picnic** in the back yard.

She needed a picnic blanket, so she grabbed one from Kari's bed.

Kari saw her stained blanket and shouted.

Mommy said,

Amy,
hold on to your horses.
Amy threw up her hands and shouted,
I'm trying!
My arms get tired.

Amy stomped to her room
and threw herself
onto her
bed.

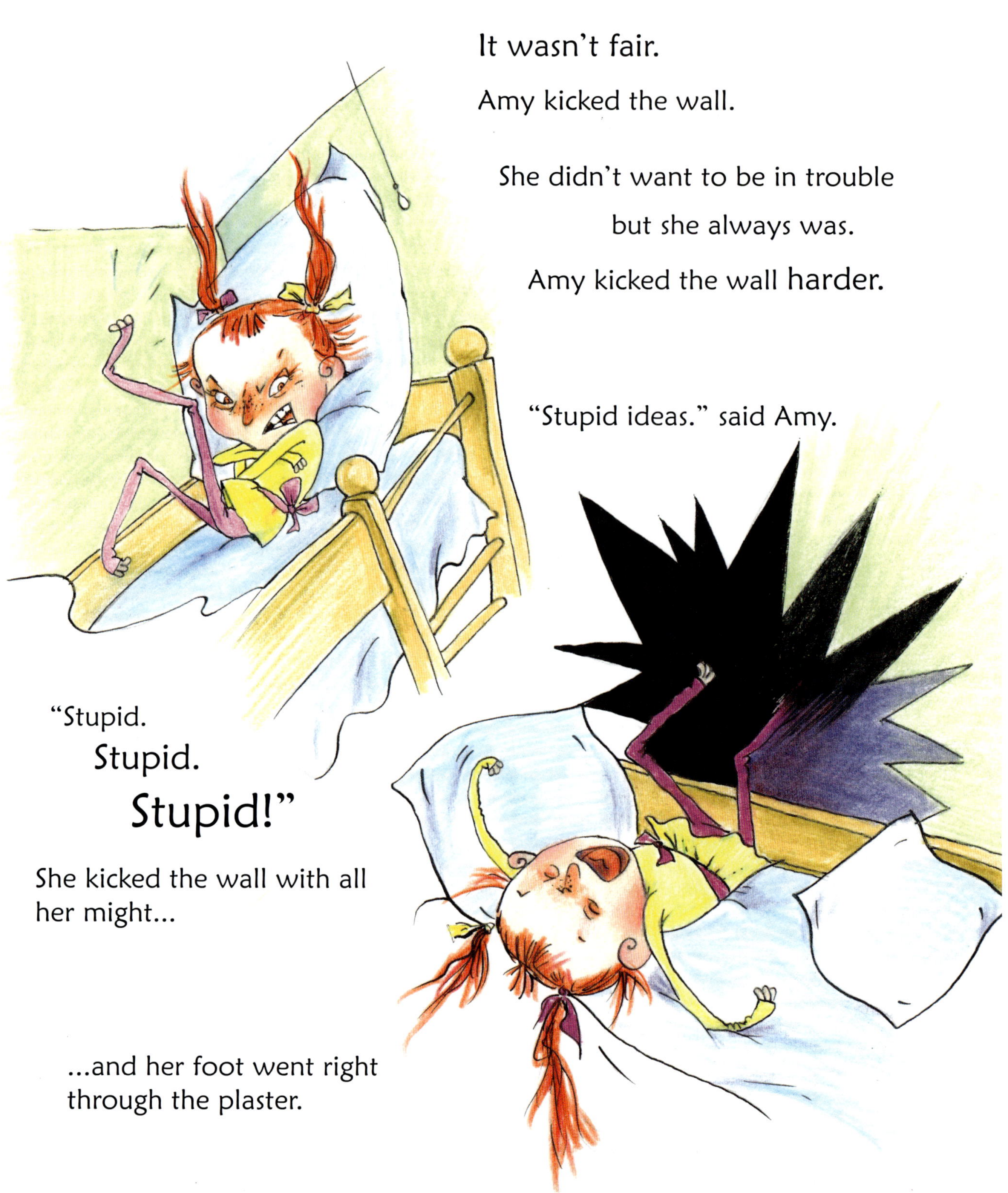

It wasn't fair.

Amy kicked the wall.

She didn't want to be in trouble but she always was.

Amy kicked the wall **harder.**

"Stupid ideas." said Amy.

"Stupid.
Stupid.
Stupid!"

She kicked the wall with all her might...

...and her foot went right through the plaster.

Amy stared at the hole in the wall.

Maybe,

if she put a pillow in front of it,

no one would notice.

Amy was very quiet for the rest of the afternoon.

All her idea horses were gone.

She was even quieter when Mommy and Daddy left Kari in charge for the evening.

Kari scowled.
"You'd better behave yourself," she told Amy.

Amy thought about the hole and nodded.

Amy did her very best to be good.

While Kari tried to do homework and Evan whined, Amy read a book.

When Kari gave up on homework and began to cook dinner,

Amy drew a picture.

Evan fussed and kicked on the kitchen floor.

Amy could hear Kari jouncing Evan on her hip and trying to calm him down, but the crying got louder.

Then there was a **crash** from the kitchen.

Amy ran to see what happened.

Everything was on the floor. Pot,
food,
broken plates,
screaming Evan,
and crying Kari.

"I can't do this!" Kari said. "Everything is ruined."

Amy peeked around the cabinet, and all her ideas came galloping back.

She knew exactly what to do.

She ran and grabbed Evan's favorite bear. She snatched a towel to mop up the spill, and a broom from the closet.

Amy swept and did a silly dance.

Evan stopped crying.

Amy made faces while picking up pieces of plates.

Evan started giggling.

Kari looked up.

Amy sang a new song about peanut butter while she made three sandwiches.

Kari took the sandwich Amy held out to her.

"It's okay," said Amy.

“Sometimes things go wrong, and we have to make them right.”

There was another thing Amy needed to make right.

Amy grabbed Kari's hand
and pulled her to the bedroom.

Amy pulled the pillow away from the hole.

"I'm sorry I broke our wall." Amy said.

"We can make this right together." Kari answered.

The next day, Kari took Amy to the store to buy a patch for the wall.

Amy paid for the patch with her own money, the clerk was surprised.

Amy smiled, “I’m little, but I’m strong.

And sometimes strong is a good thing.”

For all children whose horses have wings. --Sandra

To my boys, Yuri and Michael, without whom none of this would have been possible. --Angela

Sandra is a writer of picture books, essays, blog posts, and children's fiction. You can find her online at onecobble.com or on twitter @SandraTayler. She lives in Orem, Utah with her husband and four kids.

Angela is an artist and caricaturist with experience in illustration and political cartooning. Born in Moldova under the Soviet Union's sway, Angela currently lives in Austin, Texas with her husband and two children. You can find Angela on-line at www.arsangela.com.

Angela and Sandra would like to extend thanks to all those who backed the Kickstarter project which funded the printing of this book.

Winged Horse supporters:

Anglerfish
Marcus Adams
Colin Blair
Heidi & Jeff Creer
L.T. Elliot
Andy Ellis
Alex, Aubrey, & Janika Fulda
Edward Gowen
Chad & Sherie Mumford
Rachel & Ranae Newville
Tammy & Kambrey Owens
Harry Salzman
Jessie, Glen, Dean, & Liam Shaw
Stefan Schmiedl
Toad

Print and Original Art supporters:

Ken & Melinda Morley
Andrea Murakami
Ben Olds
David & Sarah Pascoe
MySF Reviews

For more information about *Strength of Wild Horses*, or the previous book in the series *Hold on To Your Horses*, please visit holdontoyourhorses.com